Morehouse Publishing
4775 Linglestown Road
Harrisburg, PA 17115

Morehouse Publishing is an imprint of Church Publishing Incorporated

ISBN 10 : 0-8192-4106-7
ISBN 13 : 978-0-8192-4106-1

Printed in the United States of America

Ninth Printing, 2007

CONTENTS

CONTENTS

FOREWORD

This short workbook was produced with the hope that the 1979 Prayer Book Catechism, as well as the entire book itself, would be used as the basic material for Confirmation classes.

It is hoped that by asking students to look on a certain page of the book for an answer, and, then, to write the answer down, would help the learning process. Rather than use just the Catechism, questions are designed to lead students to various parts of the Prayer Book, in order that class discussion might touch many areas of Christian life.

This workbook was designed to be used as homework—a chapter or unit per class session. Classroom time is allowed for each student to check and correct his or her own answers, and to use the questions and answers as a springboard for discussion.

It is not intended to be the sole substance of any Confirmation program, but to free teachers from producing handouts, and to free students from taking rigorous notes during class, so that both may spend more time in dialogue about the faith.

Acknowledgment is made of the work of The late Reverend George F. Kempsell who read the manuscript and provided many helpful comments.

A most grateful acknowledgment is given to my wife Debbie, who spent many hours proofreading, typing, and copying the first sets of this workbook.

Steven L. Cunningham

UNIT 1   THE OLD TESTAMENT

1. The Bible is made up of 3 sets of books. They are: (B.C.P. p. 853)

   _____ , _____ , _____ .

2. Which set shows God at work in nature and history? (B.C.P. p. 853)

   _____ .

3. Which set proclaims the Good News? (B.C.P. p. 853) _____ .

4. Why do we call the Bible, also known as Holy Scripture, the Word of God? (B.C.P. p. 853)

   _____

   _____

   _____ .

5. Read Genesis 1:1. What did God do? _____ .

6. Read Genesis 12:1-2. Who was to be the father of a great nation? _____ .

7. There came a great famine in all the lands. A famine is where there is no _____ .
   Many went to Egypt. Among these people were the descendants of Abraham. After they had

   been in Egypt many years, they were made slaves to Pharaoh, who was the _____ .

   God called _____ to tell Pharaoh to let the Hebrew slaves go. (Exodus 6:11-12)

8. When the Hebrew people had left Egypt, God gave them the 10 Commandments. What are

   they? (B.C.P. p. 847) _____

   _____ .

9. What two duties do we learn from these commandments? (B.C.P. p. 847)

   _____ , _____ .

10. Write each commandment in a short simple sentence similar to the example. (B.C.P. p. 350)

    1. <u>You shall have no other Gods.</u>   .   6. _____ .

    2. _____ .   7. _____ .

    3. _____ .   8. _____ .

    4. _____ .   9. _____ .

    5. _____ .   10. _____ .

11. In Isaiah 48:17-19, God said to the Hebrew people, "If only you had listened to my _____ ." But they had not listened. So, God sent the Messiah. What do we mean by Messiah? (B.C.P. p. 849) _____

_____ .

12. A _____ is a relationship started by God, and people respond with faith. (B.C.P. p. 846)

13. The Old _____ is the one given by _____ to the _____ people that Moses led out of Egypt. (B.C.P. p. 846)

14. On the bottom of this page write out the "Glory to God in the highest" found on page 356 of the B.C.P.

_____

_____

_____

_____

_____

_____

_____

_____

_____

_____

_____

_____

_____

_____

_____

_____

_____

_____

_____

UNIT 2   THE NEW TESTAMENT

1. The New Testament consists of books written by the people of the _____ _____ , under the inspiration of the _____ _____ , to set forth the life and teaching of _____ and to proclaim the _____ _____ of the Kingdom for all _____ . (B.C.P. p. 853)

2. What is the New Covenant? (B.C.P. p. 850) _____

   _____

   _____

   _____ .

3. Who do we believe is the Messiah? (B.C.P. p. 849) _____

   _____ .

4. Jesus' mother was _____ , and her husband was _____ . (Matthew 1:18-19)

5. What do we mean when we say that Jesus was conceived by the power of the Holy Spirit and became incarnate from the Virgin Mary? (B.C.P. p. 849) _____

   _____

   _____

   _____ .

6. When Jesus was baptized, a voice from _____ said: "This is my _____ ."
   (Matthew 3:16-17)

7. On Palm Sunday, Jesus entered the holy city of _____ , and was proclaimed as _____ of _____ by those who spread their _____ and branches of _____ along his way. (B.C.P. p. 271)

8. On Maundy Thursday, Jesus instituted (started) the Sacrament of his _____ and _____ . (B.C.P. p. 274)

9. On Good Friday, Jesus _____ on the _____ . (B.C.P. p. 276)

10. Jesus rose from the dead. On Easter Day, when the priest says "Alleluia. Christ is risen," the people say: "_____ ." (B.C.P. p. 294)

11. What is the great importance of Jesus' suffering and death? Jesus made the _____

which we could not make and we are freed from the power of _____ . (B.C.P. p. 850)

12. What is the importance of Jesus' resurrection? (B.C.P. p. 850) _____

_____

_____ .

13. Where is Jesus today? _____ .
    (B.C.P. p. 850)

14. Write the names of the 27 books of the New Testament in order.

_____	_____
_____	_____
_____	_____
_____	_____
_____	_____
_____	_____
_____	_____
_____	_____
_____	_____
_____	_____
_____	

UNIT 3   CHURCH HISTORY

1. Jesus was a Christian. True _____ False _____ .

2. The Church began at Pentecost. True _____ False _____ .

3. Christianity was illegal until the year _____ A.D.

4. From the year 313 until the _____ century, and what historians call the _____ , all of Christianity in Western Europe was under the control of the Pope.

5. Eastern Catholics broke with Western Catholics in the year _____ . English Catholics broke from the Roman Catholic Church in the year _____ , under King _____ . The _____ Church in America comes from the Anglican Church.

6. The head of the Anglican Church in England is the _____ of Canterbury. The head of the Episcopal Church in the United States is the _____ _____ .

7. The Episcopal Church authorized a new Prayer Book in 1979. It is the fourth such Book of Common Prayer, and each is known by its date of authorization by the Church. Give the dates of the four, beginning with the earliest. _____ , _____ , _____ , _____ .

8. The Episcopal Church is divided into _____ . The head of each is the _____ . What is the name of our Bishop? _____ . What diocese are we in?

_____ .

UNIT 4   THE BOOK OF COMMON PRAYER

1. The _____ _____ is the principal act of Christian worship on the Lord's Day (Sunday) and on other major Feasts. (B.C.P. p. 13)

2. In all services, everyone participates to fulfill the functions proper to their respective orders, as set forth in the _____ directions for each service. (B.C.P. p. 13)

3. The seven Principal Feasts of our Church are: (B.C.P. p. 15)   1. _____ ,
   2. _____ , 3. _____ , 4. _____ ,
   5. _____ , 6. _____ , 7. _____ .

4. Two days of fasting are observed. They are: (B.C.P. p. 17) _____ ,
   _____ .

5. The service for the Holy Eucharist, Rite One, begins on page _____ .

   The service for the Holy Eucharist, Rite Two, begins on page _____ .

   The service for Confirmation begins on page _____ .

6. By looking in the Calendar that begins on page 19, find the name of the Holy day for each date given:

   March 17 _____

   March 19 _____

   May 26 _____

   September 29 _____

   November 14 _____

   December 25 _____

7. Name the 6 seasons of the Church year (not Holy Days or National Days). (B.C.P. p. 31-33)

   _____   _____

   _____   _____

   _____   _____

8. Find the month and day for Easter in the year 1999 (B.C.P. p. 882) It will be _____
   _____ .

9. The Outline of the Faith, commonly called the _____ begins on page _____ of the Book of Common Prayer.

10. The Psalter is a body of _____ _____ .(B.C.P. p. 582) Psalm 42 begins

    on page _____ .

11. In both Rite One and Rite Two of the Holy Eucharist, the Celebrant begins the service by saying:

    "Blessed be God: Father, Son, and Holy Spirit." Then the people say: _____

    _____ .

12. Colors are used by the Church in the vestments and altar hangings and appointments. Each color represents a season or a special day, or marks a special occasion in the lives of Christians.

    Name four of these colors: _____ , _____ , _____ , _____ .

13. A priest may refuse to give communion to a person who is living a notoriously evil life. (B.C.P.

    p. 409) True _____ False _____ .

UNIT 5   PRAYER AND WORSHIP

1. What is prayer? (B.C.P. p. 856) _____

_____

_____ .

2. What prayer did Christ teach us? (B.C.P. p. 856) _____

_____ .

3. What are the seven (7) kinds of prayer? (B.C.P. p. 856) _____ ,

_____ , _____ , _____ ,

_____ , _____ , _____ .

4. What is corporate worship? (B.C.P. p. 857) _____

_____

_____

_____ .

5. During Holy Eucharist we use forms of prayer called the Prayers of the People. These begin on

   page _____ . There are _____ different forms that can be used.

6. In the Book of Common Prayer, after the Psalter, there is a section containing a variety of prayers. The prayers are numbered. Write the title of the prayer for each of the following numbers:

   #4 _____   #33 _____

   #6 _____   #43 _____

   #10 _____   #65 _____

7. When persons are sick, they can find prayers to use on page 461. Write the title of the one to be

   used if you hurt or are in pain. _____ .

8. Write the Nicene Creed (B.C.P. p. 358) on the next page.

9. Reconciliation of a Penitent, or _____ , is the rite in which one may _____

   his sins to _____ in the presence of a _____ and receive the assurance of

   _____ .

10. The _____ of a confession is morally _____ for the priest, and must not

be _____ . (B.C.P. p. 446)

The Nicene Creed

_____

_____

_____

_____

_____

_____

_____

_____

_____

_____

_____

_____

_____

_____

_____

_____

_____

_____

_____

_____

_____

_____

_____

UNIT 6   WHAT WE BELIEVE

1. What are the creeds? (B.C.P. p. 851) _____

   _____ .

2. How many creeds does this Church use in its worship? (B.C.P. p. 851)

   The _____ Creed and the _____ Creed.

3. What is the Trinity? (B.C.P. p. 852) _____

   _____ .

4. Who is the Holy Spirit? (B.C.P. p. 852) _____

   _____

   _____ .

5. How do we recognize the truths taught by the Holy Spirit? (B.C.P. p. 853) _____

   _____ .

6. What is the nature of God revealed in Jesus? (B.C.P. p. 849) _____

   _____ .

7. Sin is the seeking of _____ _____ _____ instead of the

   will of God. It has power over us because we lose our _____ .

   _____ is the act of God which sets us free from the power of evil, sin and
   death. (B.C.P. p. 848-849)

8. How can we share in Jesus' victory over sin, suffering, and death? (B.C.P. p. 850) _____

   _____ .

9. Write out the long sentence that begins "Holy and Gracious Father:" and ends with the word
   "all," found on page 362. Put it on the next page.

10. The Church is the _____ of the New Covenant. It is described as the _____

   _____ of which Jesus Christ is the _____ and of which all _____

   persons are members. In the creeds the Church is described as _____ , _____ ,

   _____ , and _____ . The Church is one because it is one

   _____ . The Church is holy, because the _____ _____

16

dwells in it. The Church is Catholic because it proclaims the _____ _____

to _____ people. The Church is Apostolic because it continues in the teaching and

fellowship of the _____ . (B.C.P. p. 854)

Answer to Question 9

_____

_____

_____

_____

_____

_____

_____

_____

_____

_____

_____

_____

UNIT 7   SACRAMENTS

1. Write, in your own words, what a sacrament is. (B.C.P. p. 857) _____

_____

_____ .

2. Write, in your own words, what grace is. (B.C.P. p. 858) _____

_____

_____ .

3. The two great sacraments of the Gospel are: (B.C.P. p. 858) _____

_____ and _____ .

4. What are the 5 other Sacramental Rites? (B.C.P. p. 860) _____ ,

_____ , _____

_____ , _____ .

5. How do they differ from the two sacraments of the Gospel?   Although they are means of

_____ , they are not necessary for _____ persons. (B.C.P. p. 860)

6. Sacraments _____ our present hope and _____ its _____
   fulfillment. (B.C.P. p. 861)

7. Ordination is the rite in which God gives _____ and the _____ of the

   Holy Spirit to those being made _____ , _____ , and _____ .
   (B.C.P. p. 860)

8. Holy Scripture and ancient Christian writers make it clear that from the _____ time,

   there have been different ministries within the _____ . Since the time of the _____

   _____ , three distinct _____ of _____ ministers have been

   characteristic of Christ's holy catholic Church. First there is the order of _____ who

   carry on the apostolic work of _____ , _____ , and _____

   the Church. Secondly, there are the _____ , or ordained elders, known also as

   _____ . With the bishop, they take part in the _____ of the Church, in

   _____ out its missionary and pastoral work, in _____ the Word of God, and in _____ his holy _____ . Thirdly, there are _____ who

assist _____ and _____ in all of this work. It is also part of their job to

minister in Christ's name to the _____ , the _____ , the _____

and the _____ . (B.C.P. p. 510)

9. Persons chosen and recognized as being called by God to the ordained ministry are admitted by

solemn _____ and the laying on of _____ _____ . (B.C.P.
p. 510)

10. Unction of the sick is the rite of _____ the sick with _____ , or the laying

on of _____ , by which God's grace is given for the _____ of spirit,

_____ , and _____ . (B.C.P. p. 861)

11. Find the page in the Book of Common Prayer that gives the prayers to be used when doing the

things in question #10. _____ .

12. Holy Matrimony is Christian _____ , in which the woman and man enter into a

_____ - _____ union, make their _____ before God and the

Church, and receive the _____ and _____ of God to _____
them keep their vows. (B.C.P. p. 861)

13. The service for the celebration and blessing of a marriage begins on what page in the Book of

Common Prayer? _____ .

14. The marriage ceremony must be attested by at least _____ witnesses, and the marriage

must conform to the _____ of the State and _____ of this Church.
(B.C.P. p. 422)

UNIT 8   THE HOLY EUCHARIST

1. The Holy Eucharist is the _____ commanded by _____ for the _____ remembrance of his _____ , _____ , and _____ _____ , until his coming again. (B.C.P. p. 859)

2. By what other names is this service known? (B.C.P. p. 859) _____ _____ , _____ _____ , _____ _____ , _____ , and _____ _____ .

3. The outward and visible sign in the Eucharist is _____ and _____ . The inward and spiritual grace in the Holy Communion is the _____ and _____ of _____ given to his people and received by _____ . (B.C.P. p. 859)

4. The benefits we receive are the _____ of our _____ , the strengthening of our _____ with Christ and _____ _____ , and the _____ of the heavenly _____ . (B.C.P. p. 859)

5. When we come to the Eucharist, it is required that we should _____ our lives, _____ of our sins, and be in _____ and _____ with all people. (B.C.P. p. 860)

6. How often should a person receive communion if they could go to church at any time? Every:

   Hour   Day   Week   Month   Year

7. To remain a member in good standing of this Church, one must receive communion _____ a year. (I.16.3. Canons)

8. Read Matthew 26:26-28. Read Mark 14:22-24. Read Luke 22:19-20. Read I Corinthians 11:23-26.

   All of these passages describe a sacrament. Which one? _____ .

9. On what page in the Book of Common Prayer, for the Holy Eucharist: Rite Two, do we find the very same words as found in the Bible in question 8? _____

10. During the Holy Eucharist, we say a short poem that proclaims the mystery of our faith. Write it on these 3 lines. (B.C.P. p. 363)

_____

_____

_____

11. On page 400 there is an outline for the Celebration of the Holy Eucharist. There are 8 essential parts. Write their titles on the lines below.

_____

_____

_____

_____

_____

_____

_____

_____

12. Any of the sacrament remaining should be _____ . (B.C.P. p. 401)

13. In class we will take this sheet to the altar and find out what these things are called, and what they are used for.

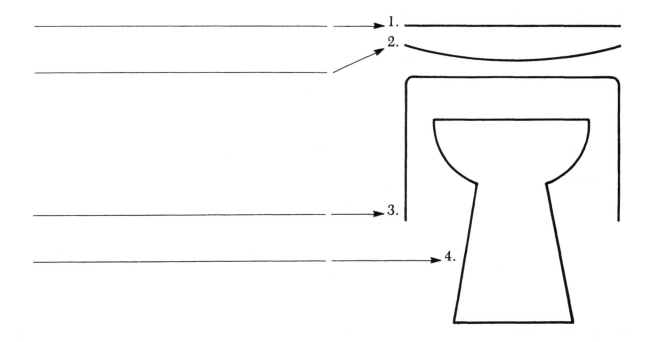

UNIT 9   BAPTISM AND CONFIRMATION

1. Holy Baptism is the _____ by which God _____ us as his children and

   makes us _____ of Christ's Body, the _____ , and inheritors of the

   _____ of God. (B.C.P. p. 858)

2. The outward and visible sign in Baptism is _____ in which the person is baptized in

   the Name of the _____ , and of the _____ , and of the _____

   _____ . The inward and spiritual grace is _____ with Christ in his death

   and resurrection, _____ into God's family, the Church, _____ of sins,

   and new _____ in the Holy Spirit. (B.C.P. p. 858)

3. What is required of us at Baptism? (B.C.P. p. 858) _____

   _____

   _____ .

4. The bond which God establishes in Baptism is _____ , which means permanent and
   forever. (B.C.P. p. 298)

5. There are two ways to baptize a person (two ways of using the water). The rubrics on page 307

   describe both ways. They are: _____

   and _____ .

6. In case of emergency, any _____ person may administer Baptism. Using the name of

   the person to be baptized you would pour _____ on that person and say _____

   _____

   _____ . (B.C.P. p. 313)

7. Any person who administers #6 should inform the _____ , so that the fact can be

   properly _____ . (B.C.P. p. 314)

8. Confirmation is the rite in which we express a mature _____ to Christ, and

   receive _____ from the Holy Spirit through _____ and the laying on of

   _____ by a _____ . (B.C.P. p. 860)

9. The service for Confirmation begins on page _____ of the Book of Common Prayer.

10. When the Bishop asks: "Do you renew your commitment to Jesus Christ?" you will say: _____

_____

_____ . (B.C.P. p. 415)

11. Read Acts 8:14-17. What sacrament is being described? _____ -

_____ .

12. All study and learning about the Church can stop when a person is confirmed, because they have

made it into the Church. True _____ False _____ .

13. When did you become a member of the Church? (B.C.P. p. 858) _____

_____ .

SUPPLEMENTAL UNIT

1. When we die, we will each become an angel. True _____ False _____ .

2. Bad angels are known as _____ .

3. The devil is an angel. True _____ False _____ .

4. There are no angels in the Bible. True _____ False _____ .

5. There is no such thing as a real witch, demon, or evil spirit. True _____ False _____ .

6. The Church consists only of the people living on earth. True _____ False _____ .

7. Do good people go directly to heaven when they die? Yes _____ No _____ .

8. At the end of the world, there will be a big war in heaven, the devil will be conquered, a new life with Christ will begin, and we will get new bodies. True _____ False _____ .

9. We never mention angels during the celebration of the Eucharist. True _____ False _____ .

10. There are no witches in the Bible. True _____ False _____ .

11. Hallowe'en has no connection with anything to do with the Church. True _____ False _____ .

13822